American Folk Tales are colorful tales of regional origin full of the local flavor and grass roots humor of special people and places. Coming from all areas of the United States, these stories provide entertaining reading material as well as insight into the customs and backgrounds of the regions from which they spring.

Distinctive color illustrations complement the text and add to the reader's enjoyment.

THE ADVENTURES OF

HIAWATHA

by Virginia Frances Voight

illustrated by Gordon Laite

GARRARD PUBLISHING COMPANY
CHAMPAIGN, ILLINOIS

THE ADVENTURES OF HIAWATHA

As Indians count the years, Hiawatha was eight summers old. He lived with his grandmother, Nokomis. Behind their wigwam swept a dark forest of pine trees. Before it, the blue waters of a great lake danced and sparkled. The Indians from the nearby Ojibway village called the lake Gitche-Gumee. In their Indian language, this meant Shining-Big-Sea-Water.

Hiawatha could not remember his mother. She had died soon after he was born. Her name, Wenonah, sounded to him like the sighing of the wind in pine trees.

Hiawatha had never seen his father, Mudjekeewis. But he knew that he was a great chief who lived in faraway Sunset Land. Indians everywhere both loved and feared Mudjekeewis, for he had power greater than that of ordinary men. He was the West Wind, and he ruled over all the winds that blew.

"When I grow up," Hiawatha said to his grandmother, "I will go to see my father."

"It will be a long journey," she said, shaking her head.

Nokomis herself had once made an even longer journey.

She had grown up on the moon where her father was Chief of the Moon People. One day Nokomis made a swing of grape-vines. On her leafy swing, she flew gaily out over the edge of the moon and high into the starry sky. Suddenly, the vine rope parted. Nokomis shot downward like a falling star. She landed unhurt near the Shining-Big-Sea-Water.

Since then, Nokomis had lived on earth. But she still had the magic of the Moon People.

On summer evenings, while fireflies danced and moonbeams rippled on the lake, Nokomis would tell Hiawatha stories.

When flowers fade on earth, she said, their colors bloom again in the rainbow. She told him that the Milky Way is the pathway of ghosts across the sky. And when Northern Lights flash and glow, it means that ghost warriors are dancing with their plumes and war clubs.

"Hoo, Hoo, Hooo," called haunting voices from the shadowy woodland. They made Hiawatha shiver.

"Ghost spirits are calling to us," he whispered.

"No. It is the owl people talking together in their own language," Nokomis said. "Listen carefully to all the birds, little one. You must learn to understand what they are saying."

Hiawatha listened to the owls and to the wild goose, Wawa. He talked to Shuh-shuh-gah, the blue heron, when the tall bird came wading along the shore. He called to the gulls as they flapped above the waves. He laughed when the noisy gulls screamed back greetings to him.

He laughed because suddenly he found
that he could talk to birds and animals.
And he could understand them when they
answered him. But how could this be?
None of the other Indian children could
talk with the wild creatures! Hiawatha
decided that his grandmother must have
passed some of her magic on to him.

As he grew older, he realized that
there were many ways in which he was

different from other boys. He was much
stronger than the others. He could shoot
ten arrows and hit the mark with every
one, while other boys were still taking
aim with their first arrow.

And when they ran races, some power
put wings on Hiawatha's feet. He always
won! Was this because he was the son
of the West Wind?

Was it the power of the West Wind
and the magic of the moon that gave
him those strange feelings that often
tingled inside him? Hiawatha felt then
that he could accomplish anything in the
world that he set out to do.

When Hiawatha reached the age when
an Indian boy became a hunter, Nokomis
asked her friend, Iagoo, to make him a
bow.

Iagoo cut a branch of ashwood and

made a strong, wonderful bow. He used deer sinew for a bowstring. He split an oak bough to make arrows and chipped flint for arrowheads. Then he winged each arrow with feathers. He called Hiawatha and gave him the bow and a quiver of arrows.

"Go into the forest and shoot a deer," he said. "Bring fresh meat to your grandmother's lodge!"

Hiawatha's face shone with pride in his new bow. The moment that he touched it, the strange power within him flowed into it. The bowstring sang. He heard it say, "We are going to do great deeds together!"

In the forest Hiawatha followed a deer trail to the river. He hid in some bushes near a pool where deer came to drink the cool, fresh water.

He watched the trail with his keen eyes.

A pair of wide-branching antlers appeared suddenly out of the leafy shadows. A deer was stepping proudly down the trail! Hiawatha's heart beat faster. He sank silently upon one knee and notched an arrow to his bowstring.

"Fly swift! Oh fly true!" he whispered.

TWANG! The bowstring sang. The deer

leaped into the air as the arrow struck
him. Then he fell dead upon the trail.

Hiawatha's shout awoke the woodland
echoes. He had proved his skill as a
hunter!

The deer was so heavy that two strong
men would have been hard put to carry
it. Young Hiawatha slung it easily across
his shoulders and carried it home.

Now Hiawatha started to grow up fast. He became tall and straight, and he had the proud look of a chief. Nokomis sewed for him fringed leggings and a shirt of deerskin, rich with embroidery of colored porcupine quills. She made him a wampum belt. She used her magic to make for him enchanted mittens and moccasins.

"On any other man, these would be only ordinary mittens and moccasins," she told him. "But when you wear them, Grandson, wonderful things will happen."

With the magic mittens on his hands, Hiawatha found that he could smash great rocks to splinters with a single blow. And when he wore his moccasins, he could walk a mile with every step.

"Now I am ready to go to see my father," he said.

"But how will you find your way to that far land?" Nokomis worried.

"I will ask the sun to be my guide," Hiawatha replied.

He put on his moccasins and stepped across the Mississippi River. Eagle feathers slanted in his hair. His belt glittered in the sunshine. Measuring a mile with every step, he followed the pathway of the sun across the grassy plains. At last he came to the Rocky Mountains. There he saw mighty Mudjekeewis sitting on a mountaintop.

Hiawatha stared at his father in wonder. The West Wind's hair blew around his head like clouds of snow. Lightning flashed in his eyes. He was strong and fierce, but there was something gentle about him too.

Mudjekeewis knew his son at once, for

Hiawatha looked as he himself had looked in his splendid young manhood.

"Welcome, Hiawatha!" he shouted. "I have waited for you a long time."

He came rushing down from the mountaintop, boastful and powerful. "You must be almost as tall and strong as I was when I was a young brave," he said.

To show his strength, Hiawatha pulled out his mittens and tore great chunks of rock out of the mountain.

The West Wind roared with laughter. "That is child's play, Hiawatha!"

Hiawatha smashed some rocks with a blow of his fist. When his father laughed again, he became so angry that he threw pieces of rock at him. Mudjekeewis blew them back with a little puff of his breath.

But now the West Wind was angry! He blew his breath out in a stormy gust,

and a forest of tall trees crashed over the mountainside. He tore up some giant rushes and beat Hiawatha with them.

Hiawatha splintered more rocks and threw them at Mudjekeewis.

Never before had the earth been shaken by such a fight as this between the West Wind and his son! Storm winds howled. Mountains came crashing down.

At last mighty Mudjekeewis called out, "Stop, Hiawatha! Let us be friends. You cannot harm the West Wind. And I fought you only to test your strength and courage."

Hiawatha gladly made friends with his father. "I will stay with you a long time," he promised.

"No, my son," Mudjekeewis answered. "You have work to do in the land of the Ojibway.

"Long ago, Gitche Manito, the Great Spirit, promised our people that he would send them a helper. You are that helper, Hiawatha. There are terrible monsters who harm our people. You must fight them and kill them. And you will find other ways in which to help our people.

"But when your work is finished, come back to Sunset Land. Then we will live together always, and you shall help me rule the winds."

Hiawatha was very happy as he started home, for he knew that he would see his father again some day. On the way he stopped at a tepee in the country of the Dacotah Indians. Here lived the Indian who made the finest arrowheads in the world. Hiawatha offered to trade many deerskins and his wampum belt for some of the Arrow Maker's sharpest points.

While the old Dacotah chipped and pol-
ished arrowheads, Hiawatha made friends
with his daughter, Minnehaha. Her name
meant Laughing Water.

Hiawatha was enchanted by Minnehaha's
beauty and by the sound of her joy-
ous laughter. He thought how pleasant
it would be to have her with him always.

Someday, he would come back and ask
Minnehaha to be his wife.

20

When Hiawatha reached home, he found his grandmother thin and weak.

"It has been hunger-time in the land of the Ojibway," Nokomis told him. "The deer have wandered away from our woodlands. Evil spirits have kept the wild rice from ripening. And Mishe-Nahma, Chief of Fishes, has eaten all the fish in our waters. Many have died of hunger."

Her words filled Hiawatha's heart with sadness.

Hunger-time did not come often to the Ojibway. Usually there were plenty of food animals for the hunters to shoot, and the lakes and streams were full of fish. In most years, the women piled their baskets high with berries, and the wild rice hung heavy on the stalks. But then would come a time when food was so scarce that Indians died of hunger.

"There should be some way to get food so that, even in bad years, we would not starve," Hiawatha said thoughtfully.

Nokomis shook her head. "There is no way, except for men to hunt and fish and for women to gather wild plants."

Excitement glowed inside Hiawatha. Perhaps this was one of the ways in which he could serve his people!

"I will ask the Great Spirit to help us," he said.

He went alone into the forest to fast and pray.

"O Gitche Manito! Help me to find a way to feed my hungry people!"

From far away there came a sound like thunder. Hiawatha was comforted, for he believed that Gitche Manito had answered.

At sunset, a tall young stranger sprang suddenly out of the air and appeared to

Hiawatha. His green shirt and leggings were trimmed with yellow fringe. Shining green plumes nodded above his silky yellow hair.

"I am Mondamin, the Spirit of Maize," the stranger said. "Gitche Manito is pleased with you, Hiawatha, because you prayed for your people instead of asking something for yourself. Your prayer will be granted, if you are willing to fight and work for what you want. So let us wrestle together. If you overcome me, your people shall have food."

Hiawatha had fasted for seven days. He felt very weak, but he bravely accepted the challenge to wrestle with Mondamin. It seemed to him that, as soon as he touched the stranger, new strength poured through his veins. But although he strove with all his might, he was not able to overcome the Spirit of Maize!

When darkness fell, Mondamin stepped back. "I will come again tomorrow," he promised.

He vanished like mist rising from the lake.

Hiawatha threw himself down to rest. He was ready when Mondamin appeared the next day. They wrestled again, and now Hiawatha thought that Mondamin was not quite so strong as he had been the day before.

The wrestling continued for four days. Hiawatha was painfully tired, but he would not give up. On the fourth day he struggled so furiously that he threw Mondamin to the ground.

"You have conquered," Mondamin whispered. "I am dying! Strip off my plumes

and clothes, and make me a bed in the soft earth. Cover me with soil and keep the weeds away. Let the sun warm my bed and the rain fall upon it. When summer comes, you will see me come back to life. And then, Hiawatha, you will have food for your people."

Hiawatha did as Mondamin bade him. Weeks passed. Then one day Hiawatha saw some tiny green leaves pushing up out of

Mondamin's bed. By summer they had become tall, beautiful plants. They had silky yellow fringe and shining green plumes that nodded in the breeze.

"They look just like Mondamin!" Hiawatha exclaimed.

The Spirit of Maize had indeed come back to life!

When the golden ears of maize were ripe, Hiawatha and Nokomis gave a feast. All the people of the tribe were invited to eat the new food. And after that, the Indians held a Thanksgiving Feast every summer to honor the Great Spirit for his precious gift of maize.

Fields of maize spread green and fruitful around the wigwams, providing food for the entire tribe. But the Indians needed fish for food too, and they dared not fish in the Shining-Big-Sea-Water. Mishe-Nahma, the huge Chief of Fishes, lay in wait there. Any Indian who was caught in the monster's cruel jaws was never seen again!

Hiawatha knew that he must free his people from the monster in the lake. To catch Mishe-Nahma, he must get far out on the water. He thought and thought about how to accomplish this. At last the idea of building a boat came to him. No Indian before him had ever built a canoe. But the magic inside Hiawatha told him just how to go about it.

He found everything he needed in the forest. He asked a birch tree for its thick white bark, and a cedar for its branches. He begged a tamarack to give him its stringy roots.

The trees sighed and murmured sadly. But they gave their treasures to Hiawatha.

Hiawatha used the cedar to make a strong frame for his canoe. He bound the birch bark to the frame with tamarack roots. He used the golden tears of a fir tree to waterproof the seams.

When he set his birch canoe in the water, it floated like a water lily. Happiness filled his heart. All his magic had gone into this canoe and with it, the secrets of the forest and the strength of the trees. And because the canoe was enchanted, he did not need a paddle to guide it. He could steer it with his thoughts—forward, backward—fast, slow.

Now he was ready to go after Mishe-Nahma!

Hiawatha willed his canoe to take him out on the lake. Just as they were starting, a squirrel came scampering from the forest and jumped onto the bow.

"Welcome, small brother!" Hiawatha greeted him.

The squirrel's perky tail blew in the breeze as they sped across the water.

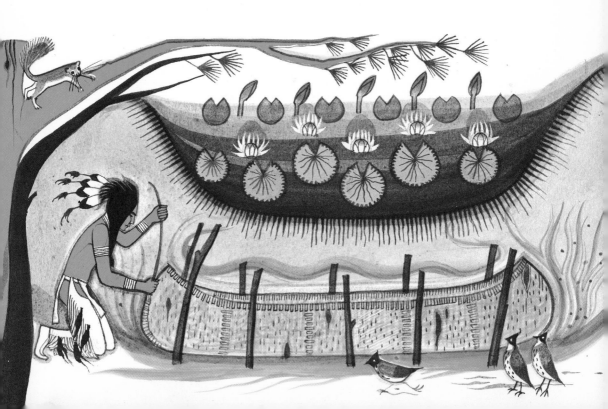

Hiawatha peered over the side of the canoe. Far down in the clear water, he could see Mishe-Nahma. The squirrel looked down also. When he saw the monster fish, his teeth began to chatter.

Mishe-Nahma was fanning the water with his purple fins. He was terrible to see with his long snout and with sharp spikes sticking out all over him. His stripes and splashes of gold, scarlet, and blue shone like war paint.

Hiawatha let down his fishing line of twisted cedar bark.

"Take my bait, O Mishe-Nahma!" he shouted. "Let us see which of us is stronger."

Mishe-Nahma glared up at the canoe. It made him very angry to be shouted at. He snapped at a pike which was swimming past.

"Go seize that rude fellow's line and break it!" he shouted.

The pike, and then a big sunfish, jerked so hard at Hiawatha's line that the canoe spun in circles.

"Go away, fish!" Hiawatha called to them scornfully. "Tell Mishe-Nahma that he is a coward. He's afraid to come near me!"

At that, Mishe-Nahma came rushing up from the bottom of the lake. He leaped high into the air and fell back with a splash that sent waves crashing against the canoe. Then he opened his great jaws and swallowed the canoe, Hiawatha, and the squirrel with one gulp!

Inside, Mishe-Nahma was like a wet black cave. Hiawatha's breath choked in his throat. How was he going to get out of the stomach of this monster? Then

he heard a cheerful chattering. The spry
little squirrel was frisking about gaily.

"I'm not afraid as long as you are
here, Hiawatha," he said.

His small friend's faith in him gave
Hiawatha new courage. Somewhere in the
darkness, he heard a thunderous beating.
It was Mishe-Nahma's heart pounding
away! Hiawatha groped about. When he
found the heart, he gave it a mighty

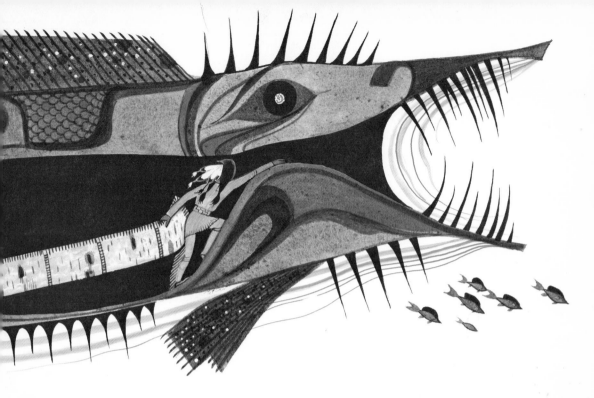

blow with his fist. The blow caused the monster to swim about wildly. Then he gave a deep gasp and died.

Mishe-Nahma was dead, but Hiawatha was still a prisoner. He tried to crawl up the monster's slippery throat, dragging his canoe behind him. The little squirrel pushed and tugged to help. But they kept slipping back.

The big waves tossed the dead fish about,

and finally, they washed it up on the beach. From his dark prison, Hiawatha heard the screaming of birds outside and the flutter of many wings.

"Ho, gulls!" he shouted. "Help me out of here!"

"It's Hiawatha!" mewed the gulls.

They tore at the fish with their beaks and claws. As soon as they had made a hole that was large enough, Hiawatha scrambled through it. He pulled his canoe after him, and the gay little squirrel rode out on the bow of the canoe.

Hiawatha thanked the gulls for helping him. Then he turned to the squirrel.

"I will give you a new name, because you have been such a cheerful little helper," he said. "From now on, boys will call you Adjidaumo, which means Tail-in-Air."

Hiawatha called Nokomis from her wigwam to see the monster Mishe-Nahma dead upon the beach.

"Our people no longer need be afraid to fish in Gitche-Gumee," he said.

Nokomis looked proudly at her hero grandson. Then her face clouded.

"But now you must fight an even more terrible monster."

She pointed far across the lake. "Yonder lives Pearl-Feather, greatest of all wizards. He casts wicked spells and sends sickness and death to us from his swamplands. Our people will never be safe while this monster lives."

"I will free them from Pearl-Feather," Hiawatha promised.

"But take care, Grandson," Nokomis pleaded. "Evil spirits lie in wait in the poisonous swamps around Pearl-Feather's wigwam. Huge serpents guard the entrance to the swamps. No Indian who has dared to venture there has ever returned."

Hiawatha laughed. "I'm not afraid of Pearl-Feather or his serpents."

He was eager to be away on another adventure.

He took his mighty bow of ashwood, his magic mittens, and his heavy war club which he had named Puggawaugun. He stepped into his enchanted canoe and patted its sides fondly.

"Take me to Pearl-Feather!"

The canoe rushed away across the lake. It was a long trip, but at last Hiawatha saw Pearl-Feather's gloomy swamplands ahead. There were the fiery serpents breathing out clouds of steam as they swam to and fro! Their thick, glittering bodies coiled and slithered on the water. They stared at Hiawatha with eyes like slits of fire. Tongues of flame shot from their mouths.

"Let me pass, O serpents!" Hiawatha called. He and his canoe looked tiny compared to the huge snakes.

The serpents rose on their tails and hissed at him, "Go back, Hiawatha! Go back, or we will kill you!"

They swam toward the canoe. Hiawatha raised his bow. The bowstring sang a wild, proud note, and a stream of arrows whizzed toward the serpents. Every arrow struck a snake. Before the serpents could reach the canoe, all of them were dead. The canoe carried Hiawatha past their tangled coils into the black, thick, evil-smelling waters of the swamp.

The swamp was a fearful place. Clouds

of mosquitoes rose from the slimy pools, singing war songs and jabbing at Hiawatha with their poisonous spears. Will-of-the-Wisps gave off a scary light. The ghosts of people slain by Pearl-Feather kept up a sad wailing. And other unearthly voices kept calling to Hiawatha, trying to get him to turn aside and become lost. But the magic canoe carried him steadfastly onward throughout the long night.

When sunrise came Hiawatha saw Pearl-Feather's wigwam of shining wampum standing on a hill. The hill was surrounded by tangled patches of water lilies and blue flags, too thick for a boat to pass through them. At a word from Hiawatha, the canoe leaped into the air and sailed over the swampy tangles, landing on the beach below the wigwam.

Hiawatha sprang ashore. His heart was beating high with excitement. He tightened the string on his mighty bow. The bowstring twanged loudly as if it, too, were glad that the battle with the wizard was near.

Hiawatha sent an arrow singing toward the wigwam. It struck the shining wampum with a resounding klunk.

"Pearl-Feather, come out!" Hiawatha shouted. "I am here to put an end to your evil doings!"

There was an angry bellow inside the wigwam and Pearl-Feather came rushing out. He was a giant, frightening to see. His face was painted for war, and his eyes were blazing with wickedness. He was clad from head to foot in wampum armor, hard as stone. He carried a war club made of a whole tree. He charged

at Hiawatha, whirling the club around his head.

"I'm going to stamp you flat and break you into pieces, Hiawatha!" he roared.

Hiawatha answered by shooting an arrow at the giant. It struck his armor and bounced back harmlessly! Hiawatha ducked under Pearl-Feather's war club and beat the wizard with Puggawaugun. The heavy blows drove the giant back a few steps. But then Pearl-Feather reached Hiawatha with a swing of his tree-club and almost knocked him down.

Hiawatha flashed away and shot arrow after arrow at Pearl-Feather. Every arrow bounced back! For the first time, Hiawatha felt a pang of doubt. What if this wizard really did have stronger magic than his own?

He ran in close and hammered at Pearl-Feather with his enchanted mittens. The mittens made only a small dent in the wampum armor.

Angry shouts and the sounds of furious blows filled the air as the two warriors stamped about and swung their war clubs. Hiawatha was bruised and breathless. His magic mittens were torn. Puggawaugun was smashed to splinters. Yet Pearl-Feather appeared to be unharmed.

42

"Now I'm going to finish you, Hiawatha!" yelled the giant. His war club had been smashed also, but he bent over to pick up a big rock.

A woodpecker had been watching the fight anxiously from a nearby tree. "Quick!" he screamed to Hiawatha. "Aim your arrows at the top of Pearl-Feather's head! It is the only place where magic does not protect him."

Hiawatha had only three arrows left. He shot them swiftly, while the giant was still tugging at the rock. They struck Pearl-Feather's head and bit in deeply. The terrible wizard Pearl-Feather fell dead!

Hiawatha drew a deep breath and leaned tiredly on his faithful bow. He looked gratefully at the woodpecker.

"I thank you, little brother."

He pulled a tuft from the eagle plumes on his own head and dipped it in Pearl-Feather's blood. Then he set the scarlet tuft on the woodpecker's head.

"Woodpeckers will wear this scarlet patch forever in memory of the help you gave me in my fight with Pearl-Feather," Hiawatha promised.

* * * * *

Brave Hiawatha had never forgotten Minnehaha. After his battle with Pearl-Feather, he told his grandmother that he was going to ask the lovely Dacotah girl to be his wife. Nokomis grumbled a little.

"Don't bring a lazy girl to our wig-wam!" she warned. "I want a grand-daughter with willing hands and with nimble feet to run upon my errands."

"Minnehaha will serve you gladly,"

Hiawatha answered. "And she will fill our wigwam with beauty and laughter."

In the tepee by the waterfall, Minnehaha dreamed often of the handsome young brave from afar. One day she looked up from her work and saw him standing in the tepee doorway. Her eyes glowed with welcome.

When Hiawatha asked Minnehaha to be his wife, she gladly put her hand in his.

All the world was bright as they walked homeward through the forest. The birds sang wedding songs. And Nokomis welcomed them with a great feast to which all Hiawatha's friends had been invited. There was storytelling, there was dancing and merriment such as Indians loved. Nokomis wore a broad smile. She was well-pleased with the granddaughter Hiawatha had brought to her wigwam.

Happy years followed. Hiawatha continued to work for his people. He showed them how to make canoes and paddles. He taught them which plants to use for medicine. He invented picture writing, so that the history of the tribe would never be forgotten.

One freezing winter day, while Hiawatha was out hunting, Minnehaha became ill with a fever. Two spirits entered the wigwam and stood beside her bed. When Hiawatha returned home, Nokomis met him with tears in her eyes.

"The spirits have taken our Laughing Water to Sunset Land," she told him.

Hiawatha gave a cry of sorrow that made the trees moan in the forest and the stars tremble in the sky.

"I will soon follow you, my Minnehaha!" he promised.

Hiawatha's work on earth was finished. He was free to go to Sunset Land where Minnehaha and his father, Mudjekeewis, were waiting for him.

He made his magic canoe ready.

Sad old Nokomis and all the people of the tribe gathered on the shore of Gitche-Gumee to see their hero go. They knew that they would never see him again on earth.

"Farewell, dear Hiawatha!" sighed the trees.

The birds sang sadly, "Hiawatha, fare-well!"

Hiawatha stepped into the canoe. "Westward! Westward!" he whispered.

The canoe moved away across the shining water. Soon it lifted into the air to float in the glowing colors of the sunset. On and on it moved until it hung like a star in the western sky. It glittered there a short time while Nokomis and the other Indians watched in breathless silence. Then it disappeared.

MEET THE AUTHOR

VIRGINIA FRANCES VOIGHT was born and raised in a reading family in Connecticut, where she now lives. She says, "My mother taught me to read at an early age, probably in self-defense, for I was always begging her to drop everything and read me a story." From reading, Miss Voight took a natural step into writing stories of her own.

In her school days she developed life-long interests in history, nature lore, and Indian lore, subjects which often appear in her books and stories. She spends most of her vacations in the Maine woods, where she finds inspiration for many animal and adventure stories.

At one point, Miss Voight considered becoming an artist, and after graduation from high school, she attended the Yale School of the Fine Arts and a commercial art school. Her more than 20 published books prove her also to be an artist of another sort—a fine author of many books for young people of all ages.

MEET THE ARTIST

GORDON LAITE has illustrated many children's stories including *John Henry*, another Garrard folk tale. After his school years at Beloit College, Wisconsin, and at The Chicago Art Institute, Mr. Laite worked in creative graphics and educational film strips. Since 1958 Mr. Laite, now a resident of Gallup, New Mexico, has been a successful free-lance illustrator. Between assignments, he is an enthusiastic gallery exhibitor. His paintings have been shown in both one-man and group shows in New Mexico and around the country.

ER MAR 1982